More Than Enough

Escaping the Trap of Scarcity Thinking

Rev. Dr. Rance Settle

Copyright © 2025 by Rance Settle
All rights reserved. No part of this publication may be reproduced, distributed, or transmitted in any form or by any means, including photocopying, recording, or other electronic or mechanical methods, without the prior written permission of the publisher, except in the case of brief quotations embodied in critical reviews and certain other noncommercial uses permitted by copyright law.

Scripture quotations are from the ESV® Bible (The Holy Bible, English Standard Version®), copyright © 2001 by Crossway, a publishing ministry of Good News Publishers. Used by permission. All rights reserved.
ISBN: 9798292159148
Printed in the United States of America

Dedication

For those who gave when it didn't make sense to give.
Who trusted God with empty jars and saw Him fill them.
Your faith is the story behind this book.

Table of Contents

Dedication 3

Introduction: The Lie of Lack...5

Chapter 1: It Starts With Trust 9

Chapter 2: The Flour That Never Runs Out 15

Chapter 3: The Myth of Not Enough 21

Chapter 4: Not Equal Gifts — Equal Trust 28

Chapter 5: This Is Not About Guilt............................. 34

Chapter 6: The Jar Is Already Full 41

Chapter 7: Legacy Starts Small................................... 48

Chapter 8: Flour, Fear, and Faith.................................55

Chapter 9: Teaching the Next Generation.................... 62

Chapter 10: Built for Eternity..................................... 69

Final Reflection: The Gratitude Habit........................76

Introduction: The Lie of Lack

There's a lie that's woven into nearly every part of modern life. It's the lie of **not enough**.

You know it well:

- *There's not enough time.*

- *Not enough money.*

- *Not enough rest.*

- *Not enough to go around.*

- *Not enough in me.*

This lie shows up when we open our calendars and feel behind before the day even starts. It whispers when we look at our bank accounts or try to find energy for one more thing. It gnaws at us when we worry that we're not doing enough for our kids, our spouse, our church, or the world. And for many of us, it even worms its way into our prayers: *Lord, I know You're good... but I don't know if it's enough.*

The lie of lack tells us that we have to hustle, hoard, and hold back. It makes us grip tighter to what little we have. It tricks us into thinking that generosity is something we'll get to *later,* when there's more margin, more stability, more cushion.

But here's the truth that cuts through the noise:

> **God doesn't start multiplying until we start trusting.**

> **He meets empty jars, empty wallets, empty hearts — with fullness.**

The widow of Zarephath was down to her last handful of flour when she met the prophet Elijah. The Macedonians were poor and persecuted when they begged Paul for the chance to give. The boy with five loaves and two fish just had a lunchbox — and Jesus used it to feed thousands.

God's economy works differently than the world's. It's not built on scarcity. It's built on **grace**. And grace is never in short supply.

What This Booklet Is — and Isn't

This is not a book about money management.
It's not a spiritual budget seminar.
It's not a guilt trip.

This is a book about **trust**.

Each chapter invites you into a biblical story where God showed up not when someone was prepared — but when they were *empty*. You'll read, reflect, and take small steps of trust. There's a "Gratitude in Action" challenge at the end of each chapter, along with questions for personal or group reflection.

Whether you use this on your own, around your family dinner table, or with a small group, my prayer is that it will open your eyes to this simple truth:

> You don't need more of what the world
> says you're missing.

You need more of the God who is already enough.

Chapter 1: It Starts With Trust

*"Bring the full tithe into the storehouse... and put me to the test,"
says the Lord.*
—Malachi 3:10

If you strip away the surface of every fear — financial fear, time fear, future fear — you'll find the same root.

Trust.

Do I trust that God sees me?
Do I trust that He will provide?
Do I trust that what I give up won't leave me empty?

Trust isn't a feeling. It's a decision.

It's what turns a jar of flour into a miracle.
It's what moves a poor widow to give two coins.
It's what caused Abraham to lay his son on an altar.

And it's where *this* journey begins — not with a budget or a calculator, but with your heart open before the Lord, asking the only question that really matters:

"Do I trust Him?"

The First Step Is the Hardest

Malachi 3:10 is one of the boldest invitations in Scripture.

God says, *"Bring the whole tithe into the storehouse... test Me in this... see if I will not throw open the floodgates of heaven."*

That's not a prosperity formula. It's a **trust test**.

God knows it's hard to let go. He knows the fear. That's why He says, *"Try Me. See what I do when you release your grip and open your hands."*

The blessing may not come in the way we expect — but it will come. Because trust never goes unnoticed by God.

Scarcity Thinking Is Fear Masquerading as Wisdom

You've heard the voice before:

- *"It's not the right time."*

- *"Be careful — don't overextend."*

- *"You've got to take care of your own first."*

And of course, God calls us to be wise stewards.

But there's a difference between godly wisdom and **fear disguised as responsibility**.

Wisdom plans for the future.
Fear hoards out of anxiety.
Wisdom asks, *"What has God provided?"*
Fear asks, *"What if He doesn't show up?"*

Scarcity isn't just a financial condition. It's a **spiritual mindset** — one that assumes God won't be enough.

But faith begins when we trust that He already is.

You Don't Need to Have Much — Just Enough to Trust

One of the greatest lies we believe is:

"I'll give when I have more."

But giving isn't about how much you have — it's about how much you're willing to trust.

Jesus never said, *"Blessed are the wealthy who give large sums."*

He pointed to the widow who gave all she had.
He told stories of small seeds becoming massive trees.
He praised people who acted in faith before they saw provision.

Because in God's Kingdom, **trust always outweighs amount**.

Obedience Unlocks Overflow

The most powerful moves of God in Scripture often followed small, quiet steps of obedience:

- Noah built the ark before a drop of rain.

- Abraham left without knowing the destination.

- The disciples cast their nets one more time after a night of failure.

God doesn't usually part the sea *before* you step into it.
He parts it *when* you trust Him enough to walk.

Obedience may feel like loss. But it's actually the beginning of abundance.

Gratitude in Action

Write down one area where you're afraid of not having enough.
Offer it to God in prayer.

Then take one small, specific step of trust this week — with your time, your resources, or your energy.

Reflection Questions

1. What area of your life is hardest to trust God with?

2. Where have you seen God show up in the past when you took a risk?

3. What voices in your life feed a scarcity mindset?

4. What's a small act of obedience you've been delaying?

5. How could your step of faith inspire someone else?

Prayer

Lord, I want to trust You more.
Help me take one bold step today.
Fill what I surrender with Your grace. Amen.

Chapter 2: The Flour That Never Runs Out

"The jar of flour was not used up and the jug of oil did not run dry, in keeping with the word of the Lord spoken by Elijah."
—1 Kings 17:16

She had already decided it would be her last meal.

The drought had dried up everything — the land, the food supply, and nearly all hope. A widow in Zarephath stood gathering sticks at the city gate when a prophet asked her for water. As she turned to oblige, Elijah made an even bolder request: "Bring me a piece of bread."

She paused. "I only have a handful of flour in a jar and a little oil in a jug," she replied. "I'm gathering a few sticks to take home and make a meal for myself and my son, that we may eat it—and die."

She didn't say it with drama. She said it with resignation. It was just the truth.

And into that truth, Elijah spoke a promise: *"This is what the Lord says: The jar of flour will not be used up and the jug of oil will not run dry until the day the Lord sends rain on the land."*

When You Don't Feel Like You Have Enough

Scarcity is not just about what's in your pantry. It's what creeps into your spirit when your strength runs out. It's what whispers when you look at the budget, or your calendar, or your energy level and think, *I've got nothing left to give.*

You feel the tug: play it safe. Hold back. Hoard your time. Protect your reserves. Wait until there's more margin, more money, more certainty.

But the call of God isn't to wait until you feel secure to trust Him. It's to trust Him **when it makes no earthly sense to do so.**

The widow didn't give out of abundance. She gave out of desperation. She didn't have enough to spare

— and yet she gave. And in doing so, she discovered that *God is not limited by what we lack.*

> That's what makes this story so powerful:
> God's provision didn't come before the act of trust — it came because of it.

God Doesn't Ask for What You Don't Have

This story echoes again in the New Testament, where Jesus praises a poor widow who drops two small coins in the temple treasury. "She gave more than all the others," He said. Why? Because she gave everything. Everyone else gave out of surplus. She gave out of faith.

Paul highlights the same kind of giving in 2 Corinthians 8 when he speaks of the Macedonian churches. These believers were going through severe trials and extreme poverty. Yet Paul writes:

> *"Their abundance of joy and their extreme poverty have overflowed in a wealth of generosity on their part"* (v. 2).

They didn't give because they were comfortable. They gave because **God's grace was already at**

work in them, turning them into people of trust. They didn't wait to have more. They gave anyway—and that's when joy broke out.

That's the paradox:

> You don't give because you have enough.
> You discover you have enough when you start giving.

Trust Is the Turning Point

There's always a hinge in these stories — a moment when faith tips forward. For the widow of Zarephath, it came when she baked that small cake of bread. For the Macedonians, it came when they "gave themselves first to the Lord." For you and me, it might come when we give up control over a budget, an anxious thought, or a tightly held excuse.

It doesn't always lead to financial abundance. But it always leads to spiritual abundance.

And just like the widow's jar, trust becomes something that keeps filling. Not in one miraculous flood, but in daily provision.

- Enough strength for today.

- Enough grace for today.

- Enough manna for today.

God doesn't promise you a warehouse. He promises you a jar.
And when you wake up tomorrow, you'll find it full again.

Gratitude in Action

Give something today that feels small but scary to let go of — time, money, control, attention, or help.

It doesn't have to be dramatic. Just one obedient step.
Then watch what God does with it.

Reflection Questions

1. Where in your life do you feel like you're running on empty?

2. What excuses do you often make to delay trusting God with your resources, energy, or time?

3. Can you name a time when you gave even though it was hard—and God showed up in a surprising way?

4. How might you teach this story (of the widow or Macedonians) to your children or someone else as a testimony of trust?

5. What's one small step you could take this week that would reflect a "jar of faith" mindset rather than a scarcity mindset?

Prayer

Lord, You know the places in my life that feel like empty jars.
 Give me the faith to trust You with what I think I can't spare.
 Help me see that Your supply is greater than my shortage. Amen.

Chapter 3: The Myth of Not Enough

"You will be enriched in every way to be generous in every way, which through us will produce thanksgiving to God."
—2 Corinthians 9:11

There's a voice that follows us into nearly every decision.

It says:

- "You can't afford to give right now."

- "You need to take care of yourself first."

- "You don't have much — and what little you have might be gone tomorrow."

It's the voice of **scarcity**.
And it sounds incredibly reasonable.

Scarcity doesn't usually shout. It just whispers softly enough to sound like wisdom. It convinces us that the faithful thing to do is to **play it safe**.

But here's the problem:
Scarcity thinking might feel smart — but it's rooted in fear, not faith.

The Myth Our Culture Loves

We live in a world obsessed with accumulation.

The world teaches us that we need **more** before we can be generous:

- More money before we can give

- More free time before we serve

- More emotional bandwidth before we invest in others

The myth of *not enough* drives everything from our advertising to our schedules. It feeds consumerism, breeds anxiety, and tells us that generosity is a luxury reserved for people who've already "made it."

But Scripture tells a different story.

> *"God doesn't ask for what you don't have. He asks for what you think you can't spare."*

When Little Becomes More Than Enough

Jesus sat near the temple treasury and watched the crowds drop their offerings in. The wealthy gave large amounts. But it was a poor widow who caught His attention — not because of the amount she gave, but because of what she held back: **nothing**.

She dropped in two small coins. Jesus said, *"This poor widow has put in more than all the others. They gave out of their wealth; she gave out of her poverty."*

God isn't impressed by amounts.
He's drawn to **trust**.

The same principle shows up when Jesus fed the 5,000. The disciples saw a hungry crowd and panicked: *"We don't have enough!"* But Jesus didn't need them to have enough. He just asked, *"What do you have?"*

A boy stepped forward with a lunch basket: five loaves and two fish. It wasn't nearly enough to feed a multitude. But in Jesus' hands, **it was more than enough**.

How the Enemy Uses Scarcity

The devil doesn't have to tempt you with wealth to derail you. Sometimes, he just convinces you that **you're poor**—even when you're not.

He makes you feel like:

- Your time is already stretched too thin
- Your finances are too fragile
- Your voice doesn't matter
- Your talents are too ordinary

Scarcity is one of the enemy's best lies. If he can convince you that what you have isn't enough, you'll never give. You'll never serve. You'll never take the first step.

But God says something radical in 2 Corinthians 9:11:

> *"You will be enriched in every way to be generous in every way."*

That means **God enriches you so you can give** — not the other way around. You don't wait until you have more. You trust, and He provides.

A Better Question: What's in Your Hands?

In Exodus 4, God calls Moses to speak to Pharaoh. Moses panics and gives a long list of excuses:

- *"I'm not eloquent."*
- *"They won't believe me."*
- *"I'm not the right person."*

And God simply asks him, *"What is that in your hand?"*

It was just a shepherd's staff. But that staff became the tool God used to part seas, perform miracles, and lead a nation.

God still asks the same question:
What's in your hand?

You don't need more.
You need to trust that God can use **what you already have**.

Gratitude in Action

This week, notice where the lie of "not enough" creeps into your thinking.
Catch it. Name it. Speak truth over it.

Then take one small action of trust — give, serve, encourage — from what you already have.

Reflection Questions

1. What area of your life do you most often believe the "not enough" lie?

2. When was a time you trusted God and gave anyway — and saw Him provide?

3. What's in your hands right now that you might be underestimating?

4. How has scarcity thinking affected your time, money, or relationships?

5. What might change if you believed you already had "more than enough"?

Prayer

Lord, I confess that I often live with a fear of not having enough.
Help me trust that You've already given me more than I see.
Use what's in my hands to bless others and glorify You. Amen.

Chapter 4: Not Equal Gifts — Equal Trust

"They gave according to their means, as I can testify, and beyond their means, of their own accord."
—2 Corinthians 8:3

We love to compare.

We compare houses, salaries, families, talents, influence.
We compare how much we give, how much we volunteer, how "spiritual" someone else seems.

But comparison is a spiritual trap.

When it comes to generosity, one of the most dangerous lies we believe is this:

"What I have doesn't matter because it's not as much as someone else."

But God doesn't measure giving by amount. He measures it by **trust**.

Faith Isn't About Equal Gifts — It's About Equal Trust

The apostle Paul writes about the Macedonian churches in 2 Corinthians 8. They were poor. They were persecuted. And yet, Paul says they gave **"beyond their means"** — not because they were pressured, but because they were filled with joy.

He doesn't commend them for the size of their gift. He commends them for the size of their trust.

That's the pattern throughout Scripture:

- The poor widow gives two coins.

- A boy gives five loaves.

- A woman breaks an expensive jar of perfume at Jesus' feet.

Each act looks different. Each gift is unique. But every one is a picture of **faith over fear**.

> The question isn't "How much did you give?"
> It's "How much did you trust?"

The Danger of Measuring Your Gift Against Someone Else's

It's easy to look at what someone else gives — or how they serve — and feel either insecure or self-satisfied.

But that's not the way of the Kingdom.

Jesus doesn't compare His disciples to one another. He calls each one **personally**. He doesn't say, *"Peter, why don't you preach like Paul?"* or *"John, why can't you lead like James?"*

He just says: *"Follow Me."*

> God never asks you to give someone else's gift.
> He asks you to give **yours**.

The sin isn't in having little or much. The sin is in **refusing to trust God with what you've been given**.

Trust Is the Great Equalizer

In Mark 12, the rich gave large gifts to the temple. No one batted an eye. It was expected.

But when a poor widow gave two small coins, Jesus stopped everything. He pointed her out to the disciples and said, *"She gave more than all the rest."*

To the world, it looked like almost nothing. To God, it was everything.

Why?

Because **she trusted Him more than she trusted her money**.

She didn't wait to be wealthy. She didn't wait until her situation improved. She gave from her scarcity, not her surplus.

And that's what moved the heart of God.

Your Faith Is Measured by Obedience, Not Outcome

Some of us resist giving or serving because we fear our contribution won't "move the needle."

But faithfulness is never wasted.

- You may never know how your prayer shaped a life.

- You may never see how your tithe impacted a mission.

- You may never hear how your service changed someone's eternity.

But God sees. God multiplies. And God honors trust.

In the end, it's not about how much you gave. It's whether you said: *"Lord, this is Yours. I trust You with it."*

Gratitude in Action

Have a family conversation about what **faithful, not flashy** giving looks like.

Talk openly about trusting God with what you have, even if it doesn't feel like much.

Reflection Questions

1. Where in your life are you tempted to compare your gifts or generosity with others?

2. When have you given something that felt small — but took great faith?

3. How does it change your perspective to know God values trust over amount?

4. What would faithful giving look like for you right now — not based on ability, but on obedience?

5. What's one thing you're holding back because it feels too small to matter?

Prayer

Lord, I want to stop comparing and start trusting. Help me give what I have, not what I wish I had. Let my offering be one of faith — not fear. Amen.

Chapter 5: This Is Not About Guilt

"Each one must give as he has decided in his heart, not reluctantly or under compulsion, for God loves a cheerful giver."
—2 Corinthians 9:7

Let's be honest.

When we hear a message about giving — especially in church — our shoulders tense up just a little. We brace ourselves for the guilt trip. The emotional pitch. The spiritual pressure.

Some of us start running mental calculations. Some of us start building defenses.

And some of us just shut down.

Because deep down, we've confused God's call to trust with a demand to perform. We've assumed that generosity is just one more thing we're supposed to do to prove we're good Christians.

But here's the truth:
Guilt can move you temporarily — but only grace can transform you permanently.

Guilt-Driven Giving Doesn't Last

You can give out of obligation for a while.

You can give because you feel bad.
You can serve because you feel guilty.
You can offer your time, money, or talents because you want to silence that inner voice that says, *"You're not doing enough."*

But that kind of giving dries up. It burns out. It doesn't bring joy. It brings resentment.

Eventually you start thinking:

- *"Why am I always the one giving?"*

- *"What difference is this really making?"*

- *"Why can't someone else step up for once?"*

That's because guilt **extracts**, but grace **invites**.
Guilt pressures. Grace draws.
Guilt manipulates your emotions. Grace transforms your heart.

The Difference Between Conviction and Condemnation

Guilt is good at dressing up like the Holy Spirit.

But there's a difference between **conviction** and **condemnation**.

- **Conviction** is a gift. It's the Spirit's way of opening your eyes to what's holding you back so you can repent, trust, and walk forward in grace.

- **Condemnation** is a lie. It says you'll never be enough, never do enough, never matter enough — so why even try?

Here's how you can tell the difference:

- Conviction leads to freedom.

- Condemnation leads to shame.

- Conviction drives you to Jesus.

- Condemnation drives you to hide.

Paul says, *"There is now no condemnation for those who are in Christ Jesus"* (Romans 8:1). That includes **how you give**. You don't give to be accepted. You give because you already are.

Gratitude Is the Engine of True Generosity

In Luke 7, Jesus is invited to a Pharisee's home. A sinful woman crashes the party, weeps at His feet, and pours out expensive perfume in worship.

The religious leaders are scandalized. But Jesus says,

> *"She loved much because she was forgiven much."*

She didn't give because of guilt.
She gave because she was overwhelmed with grace.

That's the kind of generosity God wants.

Not the kind that flows from pressure, but the kind that flows from **joy**.

You give because you've received. You pour out because you've been filled up.

And when you give from gratitude, you're not just checking a box. You're living out your identity as a beloved, redeemed child of God — free to give, not forced to perform.

It's Not About What You "Owe"

If you think stewardship is about "giving God His due," you'll always walk around spiritually in debt.

But here's the Gospel:
God isn't a tax collector. He's a Father.

He doesn't need your money. He wants your heart. He's not counting pennies. He's growing trust.

God isn't standing over you with a calculator. He's standing beside you with a cross and an empty tomb, saying:

> *"You don't owe Me. You belong to Me.*
> *Now walk in freedom."*

Gratitude in Action

Make a list of five ways God has shown you grace — physically, spiritually, relationally.

Then, from that list, choose one thing you can *give* this week as a joyful response to what you've *received*.

Reflection Questions

1. When have you felt guilted into giving or serving? What was the result?

2. How would you describe the difference between giving out of joy vs. giving out of pressure?

3. What areas of your life need to move from "obligation" to "overflow"?

4. How has God shown you grace — and how might you respond with gratitude?

5. What would change if you believed generosity was a gift, not a demand?

Prayer

Lord, I confess how often I give out of guilt or fear. Remind me that Your love is not earned, but given freely.
Help me respond with joyful trust, not pressure or shame. Amen.

Chapter 6: The Jar Is Already Full

"What do you have in the house?"
—2 Kings 4:2

We tend to focus on what we lack.

We see the gaps. The shortfalls. The limits. We fixate on what's missing — not what's already present.

But in Scripture, God consistently asks a better question:

"What do you already have?"

The Widow Who Didn't Know What She Had

In 2 Kings 4, a prophet's widow comes to Elisha in desperation.

Her husband is gone. Her debts are mounting. The creditors are coming to take her sons as slaves. She's terrified.

And Elisha doesn't offer her money. He doesn't give her a five-step financial plan.

He asks her a question:

"What do you have in your house?"

She replies, *"Nothing...except a small jar of oil."*

Except.

There's always that word. We say:

- "I have nothing... except a little time."

- "I have nothing... except this skill I don't think matters."

- "I have nothing... except this barely-there faith."

But that little jar — that "except" — was the beginning of a miracle.

Elisha tells her to gather empty jars from her neighbors, go inside, shut the door, and begin pouring.

And as she pours, the oil **multiplies**. Every jar is filled. Only when she runs out of jars does the oil stop flowing.

You Have More Than You Think

We often walk around like spiritual beggars — when we're already carrying full jars.

We forget what God has already given us:

- The presence of His Spirit
- The promises of His Word
- The people He's placed in our lives
- The gifts He's embedded in our hands

The enemy loves to keep us distracted by what we don't have, so we never use what we *do* have.

But God says:

> "You don't need to go somewhere else to find abundance.
> You need to look again at what I've already given you."

Daily Manna, Not Lifetime Storage

Part of why we feel so anxious is because we want guarantees.

We want *proof* that we'll have enough next month.
We want *certainty* that everything will work out.
We want *control* — and we call it wisdom.

But God doesn't promise a lifetime supply. He promises **daily manna**.

In the wilderness, the Israelites had to trust God every morning.
No hoarding. No saving it up for later. Just one day at a time.
And every morning — for 40 years — God came through.

He still does.

> God gives you enough for today — not tomorrow's worries.

And when tomorrow comes, He'll fill the jar again.

Open Jars, Not Closed Fists

In the miracle with Elisha, the oil only flowed when the widow was **willing to pour**.

The same is true for us.

We want God to fill us — but we often come with closed fists, guarded hearts, or a posture of fear.

But when we open the jar — when we **trust**, when we **pour**, when we **give** — that's when the supply starts flowing.

The jar doesn't look full until you start pouring. But when you do — it turns out **God has already filled it**.

You Don't Need More — You Need to See Differently

Sometimes God doesn't give us something new. Sometimes He opens our eyes to see what's already there.

Like the disciples standing next to the boy with five loaves and not realizing they already had enough.

Like Moses staring at a stick in his hand and not realizing it was the tool of deliverance.

Like you, holding a schedule, a salary, a story — and not realizing that God can use it to shape eternity.

Your jar is not empty.
It's already full.
You just haven't started pouring yet.

Gratitude in Action

Take inventory. Write down everything God has already given you — spiritually, relationally, financially, and personally.

Then circle one area where you've been saying "not enough."
How might you begin to pour from that jar in faith?

Reflection Questions

1. What's an "except" in your life that you've dismissed or downplayed?

2. When have you seen God use something small to do something meaningful?

3. What would change if you believed your jar was already full?

4. Are you trying to store up lifetime guarantees — instead of trusting God for daily provision?

5. Where is God inviting you to start pouring, even if you feel empty?

Prayer

Lord, forgive me for only seeing what I lack.
Open my eyes to the jars You've already placed in my life.
Help me trust You enough to pour — and believe You'll fill. Amen.

Chapter 7: Legacy Starts Small

"We will tell the next generation the praiseworthy deeds of the Lord, his power, and the wonders he has done."
—Psalm 78:4

Most of us don't think of ourselves as "legacy people."

That word feels big, far off, reserved for people with foundations named after them or buildings with plaques. Legacy is something for philanthropists, not ordinary families trying to pay bills and get through a busy week.

But in the Kingdom of God, **legacy isn't built with wealth. It's built with faithfulness.** And most of the time, it starts small.

The Story That Outlives You

In 2 Timothy 1, Paul writes to a young pastor named Timothy. He encourages him to be bold, to fan into flame the gift of God, to stand firm in the Gospel.

And then Paul says something beautiful:

> *"I am reminded of your sincere faith, which first lived in your grandmother Lois and in your mother Eunice..."*

Did you catch that?

The bold, gifted, Gospel-proclaiming leader of the early church was shaped not by a seminary professor or a best-selling author — but by the **quiet, steady faith** of his mom and grandma.

Their names aren't in lights.
They didn't plant churches or write epistles.
They passed down faith.
That's legacy.

> You may never see your name remembered —
> But your faithfulness might shape someone who shapes the world.

The Myth of Big Impact

We've been taught to equate legacy with scale. But in the Bible, legacy is almost always **relational, not institutional**.

- Abraham becomes the father of nations by trusting God with *one* son.

- Ruth changes history by staying faithful to *one* family.

- A boy gives a lunch that feeds *thousands* — but we don't even know his name.

God doesn't need you to change the world. He asks you to **trust Him in your corner of it**.

And when you do — He multiplies that faith in ways you'll never be able to measure.

Small Seeds, Eternal Harvest

Jesus compares the Kingdom of God to a mustard seed — the tiniest of all seeds, yet one that grows into a massive tree.

That's how legacy works.

- A bedtime prayer becomes a future pastor's calling.

- A tithe from a tight budget funds a missionary's training.

- A Sunday school lesson becomes the first time a child hears Jesus loves them.

- A generous funeral gift blesses a widow and sparks a movement.

These aren't headlines. But they're **eternal investments**.

The world may not notice.
But heaven keeps perfect books.

You Are a Living Inheritance

Psalm 145:4 says, *"One generation shall commend your works to another, and shall declare your mighty acts."*

Legacy isn't just about what you leave behind. It's about what you pass on **while you're still here**.

You are already writing your legacy:

- In how you speak about money, faith, and generosity
- In how you pray with your kids
- In how you respond when things are tight
- In how you model trust, not fear

> The question is not *if* you're building a legacy.
> The question is: *What kind?*

A Legacy of Trust

There's a moment in the Gospels when Jesus watches a woman pour out an alabaster jar of perfume at His feet — an act of devotion that shocked everyone.

Jesus says, *"Wherever the Gospel is preached in the whole world, what she has done will be told in memory of her."*

She didn't plan a legacy.
She didn't write a will or donate land.
She trusted Jesus enough to give Him her best.

And that trust became **her story.**
Her legacy.
Her offering to the next generation.

Gratitude in Action

Write a note to someone who shaped your faith — a parent, grandparent, teacher, pastor, or friend.

Then ask yourself:
What story do I want my life to tell to the next generation?

Reflection Questions

1. Who shaped your understanding of faith, trust, and generosity?

2. What acts of faith have you witnessed that left a lasting impact?

3. Where in your life might God be building legacy through small things?

4. How do you want your children (or spiritual children) to remember your walk with God?

5. What one habit or act of trust could you start now that future generations will thank you for?

Prayer

Lord, thank You for the people who shaped my faith.
Help me live today in a way that blesses those who come after me.
Let my legacy be trust in You. Amen.

Chapter 8: Flour, Fear, and Faith

"Do not be afraid. Go home and do as you have said. But first make a small loaf of bread for me... For this is what the Lord, the God of Israel, says: The jar of flour will not be used up..."
—1 Kings 17:13–14

Fear has a way of shrinking your world.

When fear moves in, risk feels irresponsible. Generosity feels foolish. Trust feels dangerous. And self-protection becomes your highest virtue.

That's what makes the widow of Zarephath's story so astonishing.

She wasn't standing in line at a bake sale. She was gathering sticks to make one final meal before death.

And into that fear — into that bleak moment of hopeless preparation — God sends a prophet with a radical request:

"Make something for me first."

It sounds absurd. Even cruel.

But it was actually the turning point.
Not just in her story — but in how God so often works.

The Real Enemy of Generosity Isn't Greed — It's Fear

We tend to think that the opposite of generosity is selfishness. But most of the time, it's not selfishness that holds us back — it's **fear**.

- Fear that there won't be enough left.

- Fear that we'll give and be forgotten.

- Fear that what we're offering is too small to matter.

- Fear that God won't come through this time.

Fear disguises itself as wisdom. It's the voice that says, *"Be careful. Hold on. Wait until things feel more secure."*

But God often shows up **right where fear wants you to shut down** — and invites you to open your hands.

> Faith doesn't start when fear is gone. Faith begins *in the middle of fear* — and keeps going anyway.

When God Meets You in the Scarcity

The widow's flour jar didn't suddenly overflow. Her pantry wasn't miraculously full.

She still had just a handful of flour and a bit of oil.

But once she poured it out in trust, **it never ran out**.

God didn't remove the tension. He showed up *in it*.

And that's how He often works.

We pray, "God, take away the fear," and sometimes He does.
But more often, He whispers, *"I'm here. Pour anyway."*

Why Fear Can Actually Be Holy Ground

In the Old Testament, when Moses stood before the burning bush, he trembled in fear. And God said, *"Take off your sandals. The place where you are standing is holy ground."*

Fear isn't always a sign that you're in the wrong place.
Sometimes it's a sign that you're standing on **the edge of something sacred**.

That's where the widow stood. That's where the Macedonians stood. That's where you may be standing right now — between what makes sense and what God is calling you to trust.

And that fear?
That ache?
That trembling?

It might be the beginning of something holy.

When the Cross Looked Like Loss

The greatest act of trust in history didn't look like victory.
It looked like surrender. Defeat. Death.

At the cross, Jesus emptied Himself fully — not with a guarantee of comfort, but with a promise of resurrection.

The disciples scattered. The sky turned black. Hope seemed buried in a tomb.

But three days later, the jar of life was full again.

> You can't have resurrection without surrender.
> And you can't have trust without risking what you can't control.

You Don't Need Fear to Go Away — You Need God to Be With You In It

The widow feared death — and found provision. The disciples feared the storm — and found Jesus asleep in the boat.

The early church feared persecution — and found the Spirit filling them with boldness.

Your fears are not too much for God. He doesn't shame you for having them. He invites you to bring them to Him.

Because He knows the truth:

> **Fear loses its grip when you start to pour anyway.**

Gratitude in Action

Write down one fear that's been keeping you from trusting or giving freely — financially, emotionally, or spiritually.

Then take one small step *anyway*. Make the call. Start the gift. Have the conversation. Pour a little flour.

Reflection Questions

1. What fears come up when you think about generosity, service, or trust?

2. Where do you see fear disguising itself as "practicality" in your life?

3. Can you remember a time God showed up *in the middle* of fear?

4. What would happen if you gave or acted *before* the fear was gone?

5. Where might God be saying, "This place of fear is actually holy ground"?

Prayer

Lord, You know the fears that whisper in my heart.
Thank You for meeting me in the middle of them — not after they're gone.
Give me the courage to trust You, even when I'm trembling. Amen.

Chapter 9: Teaching the Next Generation

"One generation shall commend your works to another, and shall declare your mighty acts."
—Psalm 145:4

If we don't teach our children how to trust God, the world will teach them how to fear everything else.

They're already learning:

- To measure success by accumulation.

- To see money as status.

- To believe that worth comes from owning more and giving less.

We don't have to be wealthy to teach generosity. We just have to be willing to model it.

Because trust is *caught* before it's *taught*. And the next generation is watching more than we realize.

Your Life Is the Lesson

You don't need a whiteboard or a financial seminar to teach trust. You just need to let your kids, grandkids, or spiritual children *see* it in you.

They notice when:

- You pray before paying the bills.
- You tithe even when things feel tight.
- You give to someone in need without expecting applause.
- You say, *"We're not buying that right now — because we're giving something better."*

Faith is taught by actions that seem small at the time but sink deep roots in the soul.

You may not remember the moment.
But they'll remember the feeling:
"In our house, we trust God first."

Visual Generosity

One of the most powerful ways to teach trust is to **make it visible**.

In Deuteronomy 6, God tells His people to speak about His commands as they walk, eat, lie down, and rise — and even to "write them on the doorposts" of their homes.

Why? Because *spiritual habits need physical reminders.*

Here are some simple, visual ways to model generosity:

- Keep an "offering jar" or "blessing box" in your home for weekly giving.

- Let your kids help choose a mission or ministry to support as a family.

- Write and display a short family giving prayer.

- Set aside time to serve together — and talk about it afterward.

These acts don't need to be big. They just need to be **consistent**.

Because small habits, repeated with love, become **a culture of trust**.

Tell the Stories

Psalm 78 calls parents to "tell the next generation the praiseworthy deeds of the Lord."

We often think of stewardship as technical. But it's also **narrative**.

Tell the story of when:

- You gave even though it felt scary.
- Someone gave to you when you least expected it.
- God showed up just in time.

- A season of scarcity turned into a testimony of abundance.

These aren't just financial moments. They're **faith moments**. And they deserve to be passed down.

Let your kids hear *why* you give — not just *that* you give.

Let them hear how much you trust Jesus — not just how much you put in the plate.

Let them see that faith isn't just for Sunday — it's for the grocery list, the budget conversation, the unexpected bill, and the offering envelope.

What They See Is What They'll Repeat

It's tempting to think our kids will "figure it out" later. But we're always forming them — whether we mean to or not.

- If they see us give out of joy, they'll learn that God provides.

- If they see us give out of guilt, they'll think God is demanding.

- If they never see us give at all, they'll assume generosity is optional.

You don't need to be perfect. Just **honest and faithful**.

Even saying, *"I'm nervous, but I trust God"* is a lesson.

Even praying together before writing a check is a seed.

Even choosing to serve instead of consume is a pattern.

The next generation is not just watching — they're learning to walk the path of trust you're paving.

Gratitude in Action

Choose one act of generosity to do *with* your child, grandchild, or someone you're discipling this week.

Let them see it. Invite them into it. Then talk about why you did it — and what it meant.

Reflection Questions

1. What did your parents or mentors model for you about generosity and trust?

2. What habits are you modeling right now — intentionally or unintentionally?

3. What stories of trust or provision could you begin telling in your home?

4. What physical reminders could you add to your daily life to make trust visible?

5. Who in your life needs to *see* your faith, not just hear about it?

Prayer

Lord, thank You for the people who taught me to trust You.
Help me be that kind of person for someone else.
Let my life be a visible story of faith for the next generation. Amen.

Chapter 10: Built for Eternity

"You will be enriched in every way to be generous in every way, which through us will produce thanksgiving to God."
—2 Corinthians 9:11

Most of what we build won't last.

The bank account will empty.
The house will need repairs.
The car will break down.
The trophies will gather dust.
The social media posts will fade.

But some things — the best things — **do last.**

When you give in faith...
When you serve with love...
When you pour out your life for the sake of Christ...

You are building something eternal.

God Doesn't Just Count Dollars — He Multiplies Trust

In 2 Corinthians 9, Paul tells the church that their generosity is doing more than paying bills or helping people — it's *"producing thanksgiving to God."*

Did you catch that?

Your giving isn't just a transaction.
It's a testimony.

It tells a story:

- That you trust God's provision.

- That your hope isn't in money, but in mercy.

- That you believe what's given in faith can ripple out into eternity.

When you give with that kind of trust, **God multiplies it.**

Not always in visible ways.
Not always in timelines we understand.
But always in ways that change lives — starting with yours.

You're Not Just Giving to Church — You're Giving Through It

It's easy to reduce stewardship to fundraising. But biblically, giving is never just about sustaining an institution. It's about **fueling a mission**.

- Every child who hears the Gospel through your church's school or Sunday school...

- Every hurting family who finds hope through your food pantry or community outreach...

- Every member who's strengthened in faith, every neighbor reached, every missionary sent...

That's not just logistics.
That's legacy.

When you give to the church, **you're giving through it** — into the lives of people you may never meet, for a Kingdom you can't fully see... yet.

Stones, Stories, and Sacrifice

Look around your church building — at the bricks, the stained glass, the altar, the pews.

Someone gave to build those.
Someone prayed for those.
Someone sacrificed so that future generations could gather, hear the Gospel, and be sent in Jesus' name.

You are sitting in someone else's legacy.

Now, it's your turn to write one.

You may not build a building. But every act of trust — every time you give, serve, teach, encourage, or pray — you are adding to **something God is building.**

> *"Unless the Lord builds the house, the builders labor in vain..."* (Psalm 127:1)
> But when the Lord builds it — and you bring your offering — the impact lasts forever.

A Legacy of Faith, Not Just Finances

The goal isn't to give more money for the sake of it. The goal is to give more **trust** to the One who gave everything for you.

Jesus didn't die so we could build a nicer building. He died to build a *Kingdom* — one that lasts. One where grace reigns. Where fear falls. Where generosity flows.

And He invites you — not just to receive it, but to **build it with Him.**

When You Give, You Preach

Every act of generosity is a sermon.

It says:

- *"God is my provider."*

- *"The Gospel is worth it."*

- *"I trust that what I give in faith will never be wasted."*

One day, you'll meet people in heaven whose lives were changed by a mission you supported, a church you gave to, a ministry you prayed for, a kid you taught, a neighbor you served.

You won't remember the amount. But God will remember the **trust**.

And that trust? It echoes through eternity.

Gratitude in Action

Write down one bold act of trust you've been avoiding.
Something you know God is prompting — a gift, a step, a sacrifice.

Pray about it. Talk to your family. Then do it.

Pour it out. Let God build with it.

Reflection Questions

1. When you think about your legacy, what do you hope it will be?

2. How does seeing giving as *mission* rather than *maintenance* change your mindset?

3. What's something in your church that exists today because someone gave years ago?

4. What are you building with your faith, time, resources, and influence?

5. Where is God inviting you to take a bold, trust-filled step toward eternity?

Prayer

Lord, thank You for those who built the legacy I now stand in.
Give me faith to build something eternal for others.
Multiply my trust into Kingdom impact I may never see. Amen.

Final Reflection: The Gratitude Habit

"Give thanks in all circumstances, for this is the will of God in Christ Jesus for you."
—1 Thessalonians 5:18

You've walked through fear.
You've stared down scarcity.
You've remembered the flour, the jar, the oil, the cross.

You've heard God whisper again and again:

> *"Trust Me. I've given you more than enough."*

But now what?

What happens after the booklet is closed...
After the sermon series ends...
After the offering plate is passed?

The answer is simpler than you think:

> You form a habit.
> Not of giving.
> Not of doing more.
> But of **gratitude.**

Gratitude Keeps the Jar Open

You don't need to feel generous to be generous.
You don't need a breakthrough to begin.

You just need to wake up each day and say:

> *"Everything I have comes from the Lord. I'll hold it with open hands."*

That's what gratitude does.
It takes what we've learned — about trust, faith, and provision — and turns it into a posture we live from, not just a moment we remember.

Gratitude doesn't start when the circumstances improve.
It starts in the middle of the unknown.

It's what the widow felt when the jar didn't run out. It's what the Macedonians lived even in poverty. It's what the early church practiced as they gave joyfully, even under pressure.

And it's what God calls *you* to walk in — one day at a time.

Scarcity Is a Cycle — So Is Trust

Scarcity thinking will try to creep back in. That whisper of "not enough" may return. Fear will knock again.

But now, you know what to do:

- Name it.

- Pray through it.

- Take one small step of generosity in the other direction.

Each time you do, you break the cycle of fear. And you reinforce the rhythm of **trust**.

You Don't Graduate From Trust — You Grow In It

This journey doesn't end. That's the good news.

You will have new seasons. New jars. New opportunities.
But you will *never* run out of reasons to trust the God who fills emptiness with abundance.

So keep opening your hands.
Keep pouring.
Keep living like Jesus is worth it.

Because He is.

Final Gratitude in Action

Start a simple habit of daily gratitude.

Each morning, write down one thing you're thankful for and one way you will trust God that day — with your time, your money, your presence, or your heart.

Watch how trust becomes second nature.

Final Reflection Questions

1. What's the biggest shift in your thinking after this journey?

2. What habits can you build into your life to keep trust growing?

3. Where is God inviting you to live with open hands?

4. How will you keep the "gratitude habit" alive in your home or heart?

Final Prayer

Lord, thank You for filling my life with Your grace. Help me live with open hands, trusting You with everything I have.
Let gratitude be more than a feeling — let it be my way of life. Amen.

MY COVENANT OF GRATITUDE

"Each one must give as he has decided in his heart... for God loves a cheerful giver."

GOD HAS GIVEN EVERYTHING – EVEN HIS OWN SON. TODAY, I RESPOND TO HIS GENEROSITY NOT WITH GUILT, BUT WITH GRATITUDE. I CHOOSE TO TAKE A STEP OF FAITH AND LIVE OUT MY TRUST IN HIM.

MY STEP OF FAITH IN GIVING

- ☐ I AM BEGINNING A HABIT OF REGULAR GIVING – I'M READY TO STOP WAITING FOR "SOMEDAY" AND START TRUSTING NOW.
- ☐ I COMMIT TO CONSISTENT, PERCENTAGE-BASED GIVING – A MEANINGFUL PORTION OF WHAT GOD PROVIDES.
- ☐ I'M PRAYING AND WORKING TOWARD GIVING A FULL TITHE (10%) IN THIS NEXT SEASON OF FAITH.
- ☐ I ALREADY TITHE AND AM ASKING GOD TO GROW MY GENEROSITY BEYOND THE TITHE FOR THE SAKE OF THE MISSION

💡 TRY GIVING UP ONE MEAL OUT A WEEK AND REDIRECTING THAT MONEY AS AN OFFERING OF GRATITUDE. GOD DOES NOT ASK US TO GIVE WHAT WE DON'T HAVE – HE'S ASKING US TO TRUST HIM WITH WHAT WE THINK WE CAN'T SPARE

OTHER STEPS I'M TAKING

- ☐ I COMMIT TO REGULAR WORSHIP WITH MY CHURCH FAMILY.
- ☐ I WANT TO GROW IN COMMUNITY THROUGH A SMALL GROUP OR BIBLE STUDY.
- ☐ I'M WILLING TO SERVE WHERE GOD NEEDS ME.
- ☐ I WANT TO EXPLORE LEGACY GIVING (ESTATE GIFTS, SPECIAL OFFERINGS).

Made in the USA
Coppell, TX
29 August 2025

53782555R10046